Freddie Me

Sandra Woodcock

Published in association with The Basic Skills Agency

Hodder & Stoughton

A MEMBER OF THE HODDER HEADLINE GROUP

Acknowledgements

Cover: Camera Press

Illustrations: pp 2, 10 All Action; p6 Hulton Getty; pp 18, 22, 24, 26 Redferns

Every effort has been made to trace copyright holders of material reproduced in this book. Any rights not acknowledged will be acknowledged in subsequent printings if notice is given to the publisher.

Orders; please contact Bookpoint Ltd, 39 Milton Park, Abingdon, Oxon OX14 4TD. Telephone: (44) 01235 400414, Fax: (44) 01235 400454. Lines are open from 9.00–6.00, Monday to Saturday, with a 24 hour message answering service.
Email address: orders@bookpoint.co.uk

British Library Cataloguing in Publication Data
A catalogue record for this title is available from the British Library

ISBN 0 340 77618 8

First published 2000

Impression number   10 9 8 7 6 5 4 3 2 1
Year   2005 2004 2003 2002 2001 2000

Copyright © 2000 Sandra Woodcock

Typeset by GreenGate Publishing Services, Tonbridge, Kent.
Printed in Great Britain for Hodder and Stoughton Educational, a division of Hodder Headline Plc, 338 Euston Road, London NW1 3BH, by Redwood Books, Trowbridge, Wilts

Contents

1 Early Life

The name Freddie Mercury is famous in rock music.
But it was not a real name.
Freddie was born on the island of Zanzibar
on 5 September 1946.
His real name was Faroukha Bulsara
and his parents came from Bombay in India.
He had one sister called Kashmira
who was born in 1952.

When he was eight years old,
the family moved back to India.
Faroukha was a bright boy
and his father wanted him to do well at school.
He sent him to a boarding school
fifty miles from Bombay.

It was an English boarding school.
It was there that he took the name Freddie.
He never went back to using his real name.

The school was quite strict.
Freddie said he grew up very quickly.
There was a lot of sport.
Freddie liked boxing and table tennis best.

When he was ten
he was school champion at table tennis.
He was so good he would play left handed
with the right hand tied behind his back.

His best subject at school was Art.
He also liked music.
He liked to listen to the singer Lata Mangeshkar.
She was one of India's top singers.
Freddie sang in the school choir
and he learned to play the piano.

Freddie left school with good exam results
in English, History, Art and Music.
In 1963 the family moved to England.
Freddie went to college in London to study Art.

He liked London in the 'Swinging Sixties.'
He did not want to stay at home with his parents
so he found a tiny flat in Kensington.

Freddie Mercury

He took part time jobs in the holidays.
He did washing up at Heathrow Airport
and stacking crates in a factory.

People made fun of him
because of his unusual looks and his posh accent.
But Freddie had great charm
and could always win people round.
He was witty and often made fun of himself.

He passed his Art course with grade A
and went on to study graphic design
at Ealing College.
Freddie was a big fan of Jimi Hendrix.
He did paintings and drawings of him
and hung them on all the walls of his flat.
He still loved music and mixed
with other students who
played and sang in bands.

He wanted to be the front man
in a band of his own.
His parents did not like
the idea of show business.
They wanted him to have a proper job.
Freddie spent less and less time with them.
He had many friends and
they remember him saying
'I'm not going to be a star.
I'm going to be a legend'!

But he still worked hard
and in 1969 he gained a Diploma
in Graphic Art and Design.
He tried looking for a job
but he had bought a second-hand guitar.
He was learning to play
and he was writing songs.

Queen Live 1975

2 Getting Started

Freddie was hired as a singer
for a rock group called *Ibex*.
His friends, Roger Taylor and Brian May
had formed a group called *Smile*.

Freddie and Roger Taylor set up a market stall
selling good second-hand clothes.
Freddie liked dressing up
and would wear big hats, feather boas
and paint his nails black.

With *Ibex* he went all over England
playing in clubs.
He wore tight satin trousers, lace shirts,
gold capes, feathers and fox furs.
All his outfits were extreme.

This didn't go down very well with some people.
But on stage he stood out from any other act.
He marched and stomped up and down the stage.
He could sing and he was a great performer.

Freddie was sharing a flat
with Roger Taylor and Brian May.
In April 1970 they decided
to start a group of their own.

Freddie wanted to call the group *Queen*.
The other two were not sure.
Brian May said people would laugh at them.
But Freddie won them over.
They took the name *Queen*.
Freddie also changed his own surname
from Bulsara to Mercury.
He wanted a new start to his life.

The new band needed a bass guitar player.
It took six months to find someone.

Queen played their first concert at
Imperial College in London.
It went well.
They were playing to friends
and other students.
Queen had two bass players
before they found John Deacon.
When he joined them, *Queen* was complete.

Queen signed their first recording contract
with Trident and then with EMI.
Their first album came out in July 1973.
It was called 'Queen'
The group soon had many fans.

Performing with *Queen* Wembley Arena 1984

Freddie wrote songs
and was the star performer in the group.
He was a good front man.
He had a good singing voice with a wide range.
His stage shows were always lively to watch
and his outfits were always extreme.

The fans wanted more of their music.
But the music press seemed to hate them.
Freddie always got a bad deal from the press.
They couldn't make up their minds
whether he was gay or just pretending to be.

Freddie teased them.
He wouldn't give a straight answer.
It was none of their business.
Queen's music got bad reports in the music press.
The *Record Mirror* said they were
'the dregs of rock and roll'.

There were worse insults
for Freddie and his gimmicks.
He shaved his chest, he wore drag,
he posed and preened in skintight catsuits.
He was always shocking.
But the fans loved him.
Every concert was a sell-out.

3 Success

Queen went to Europe and to Australia.
They toured America.
They made more albums.
Queen II and *Sheer Heart Attack* came out in 1974.
They started to make a lot of money.

They went to Japan and were mobbed by fans.
At their first concert in Japan,
there were 30 Sumo wrestlers
to keep the fans from the stage
It didn't work.
A wave of teenage girls swept past them.
But when Freddie put up his hand
to wave them back,
they all went back to their seats.

In 1975 *Queen* started a new trend.
They released a video to promote a new single.
It was the first time a video had been made
to promote a pop song.
The song was *Bohemian Rhapsody*.
It was from the new album *A Night at the Opera*.

It was a very different style of pop song.
It was like mock opera.
It had taken three weeks to record.
It was almost six minutes long.

Everyone said the song was too long
to make it as a hit.
Freddie would not agree to cut it down
to the usual three minutes.
He said 'It stays as it is or forget it'.
It could have been a flop, but it was a great hit.
Fans loved it. They called it *Bo Rap*
and it won many new fans for *Queen*.

It was played by all the radio stations.
As usual the music press slammed it.

Queen stood out as a new exciting group.
By the end of 1975
they were the biggest band in Britain.
The band wanted to say thank you to all their fans.
So they held a big concert in Hyde Park in London.
It was free to all who wanted to come.
200,000 fans turned up.
It was the biggest concert ever in Hyde Park.

Queen went on to make more albums.
They won awards for their music.
They made hit songs like *We are the Champions*.
It has become a top song with football fans.

They still shocked people with their ideas.
When they were making the album *Jazz*,
they hired Wembley Stadium
and fifty naked girls had a bike race.
A photo of the rear view was on the record cover.
There were protests in many countries
and pants were drawn on the girls!

Queen were very busy.
They made more albums, did music for films
and toured South America.
They had many top singles
in countries all over the world.
Some of their top hits were –
I Want to Break Free, Radio Gaga
and *Another One Bites the Dust.*

Many music critics still sneered at them.
Freddie was the one they mocked
because of his stage gear and his style.
One music magazine asked
'Is this man a prat?'

Freddie said they could not perform
their kind of music in boring jeans and t-shirts.
The others in the band went along with him
and dressed in drag too.

But Freddie was always the most daring.
He changed his style from ballet costume
to leather and chains.
He cut his hair and grew a moustache.
He was always bold and brazen.

Wembley Arena 1984

4 Lifestyle

Freddie always worked hard
and he made a lot of money.
He knew how to spend it as well.
Freddie wanted to enjoy his success.
He spent a fortune enjoying himself.
He could have anything he wanted.

His parties were famous for being 'over the top'.
At one party there were mud wrestlers,
topless waitresses, fire eaters,
dwarves and Zulu tribesmen.
Another time, he paid for all his friends in London
to fly by Concorde to his birthday party in America.

He was living an extreme lifestyle.
He had casual affairs with gay men.
He had women lovers too.
But Freddie was very lonely inside.
In one interview he said,
'Can you imagine how terrible it is
when you have got everything
and you are still desperately lonely?'

There were many ups and downs in his life
but one woman was his friend for all time.
She was Mary Austin
and he called her his soul mate.
He met Mary when he was a student in London.
She was always there for him.

5 Live Aid

In 1985 there was a terrible famine in Ethiopa.
The world was shocked to see
people dying of hunger on their TV screens.
The pop star, Bob Geldof,
planned a huge concert in Wembley Stadium
to raise money for the famine.
It was a world event.
Many top stars and bands were invited to perform.
Queen were invited.

The concert took place on July 13
and *Queen* stole the show.
Freddie was at his very best.
He was the heart and soul of the event.

Even top performers like Elton John,
David Bowie and Madonna
could not compare with him.
The concert was watched
by 2 billion people across the world.
It raised a lot of money.
Even the press was full of praise for Freddie.

Live Aid

6 Solo Projects

Freddie had his great success with *Queen*.
But he liked to try solo projects as well.
He did an old song called
The Great Pretender in his own style.
It was a hit.

He also surprised many people
when he teamed up with an opera singer.
Freddie had always liked opera.
He admired a Spanish singer
called Montserrat Caballe.

She worked with him on a song called *Barcelona*.
They sang it together in the city of Barcelona
when the Olympic Games were held there in 1988.
The two singers became great friends.

With the opera singer Montserrat Caballe

7 A Sad End

1987 was a sad year for Freddie.
He found out that close friends had Aids.
Some of them were dying.
The newspapers were full of it.
The Sun had a headline
AIDS KILLS FREDDIE'S LOVERS.

Other newspapers wrote about
Freddie's visits to a clinic in London.
Freddie denied that he had Aids.
He carried on working. He looked OK.
But in the next few years,
Freddie did become ill.

He started to look tired and weak.
There were strange dark marks on his skin.
He was not seen out and about.

Queen did not tour as they used to do.
Instead, they released videos
to promote their new album.
The public saw less and less of Freddie.
He was leading a very quiet life now.

Freddie Mercury looks ill at the Brit Awards

At the start of 1991,
Freddie was looking very ill.
He had lost a lot of weight
and he was in pain.
But still he made himself work.

In May, the band made the video
Days of Our Life. It was their last one.
The press were hounding Freddie
to find out if he had Aids.
He kept his illness very private.

On November 23, he was very ill indeed.
He sent a statement to say
that he did have Aids.
The next day he died at his home in London.
His family and close friends were with him.

The news made headlines
all around the world.
After his death,
there were many tributes to him
from all over the world.
A concert was held at Wembley stadium.

Freddie Mercury was a star
who was larger than life.
Many people had made fun of him.
But he always had the upper hand.

He said, 'My songs are like Bic razors …
You listen to one, like it, discard it,
then on to the next.'
Freddie only claimed to entertain.
He did that better than most.
He was a brilliant performer
and his music, his films and his memory
will live on for a long time.